$14.81

Our Neighborhood Food Drive

Extend the Counting Sequence

Corey Halloran

ROSEN
COMMON CORE MATH
READERS

Rosen Classroom™

New York

Published in 2014 by The Rosen Publishing Group, Inc.
29 East 21st Street, New York, NY 10010

Copyright © 2014 by The Rosen Publishing Group, Inc.

All rights reserved. No part of this book may be reproduced in any form without permission in writing from the publisher, except by a reviewer.

Book Design: Mickey Harmon

Photo Credits: Cover Jupiterimages/Thinkstock.com; p. 5 (boy) iofoto/Shutterstock.com; p. 5 (food) Steve Cukrov/Shutterstock.com; p. 7 Henryk Sadura/Shutterstock.com; p. 9 Monkey Business Images/Shutterstock.com; p. 11 zmkstudio/Shutterstock.com; pp. 13, 15 (cans) Markus Mainka/Shutterstock.com; p. 15 (peaches) Marcel Jancovic/Shutterstock.com; p. 17 Bombaert Patrick/Shutterstock.com; p. 19 OZaiachin/Shutterstock.com; p. 21 Ronald Sumners/Shutterstock.com; p. 22 Dmytro Mykhailov/Shutterstock.com.

Halloran, Corey.
Our neighborhood food drive: extend the counting sequence / Corey Halloran.
   p. cm. – (Core math skills. Operations and algebraic thinking)
Includes index.
ISBN 978-1-4777-2067-7 (pbk.)
ISBN 978-1-4777-2068-4 (6-pack)
ISBN 978-1-4777-2221-3 (library binding)
1. Addition—Juvenile literature. 2. Subtraction—Juvenile literature. 3. Counting—Juvenile literature. 4. Community life—Juvenile literature. I. Title.
QA113.H35 2014
513.2'1—dc23

Manufactured in the United States of America

CPSIA Compliance Information: Batch #CS13RC: For further information contact Rosen Publishing, New York, New York at 1-800-237-9932.

Word Count: 280

Contents

Jamarie Gives Back	4
Getting People to Help	8
Sorting the Food	12
Sending It Off	18
Glossary	23
Index	24

Jamarie Gives Back

Jamarie likes to help people in need.

Some people have no food.

One way to help is to have a food drive.

That's when people gather food to give others.

5

Jamarie gathers food from houses nearby.

There are 15 houses on his street.

There are 21 houses on other streets around it.

There are 36 houses in his **neighborhood**.

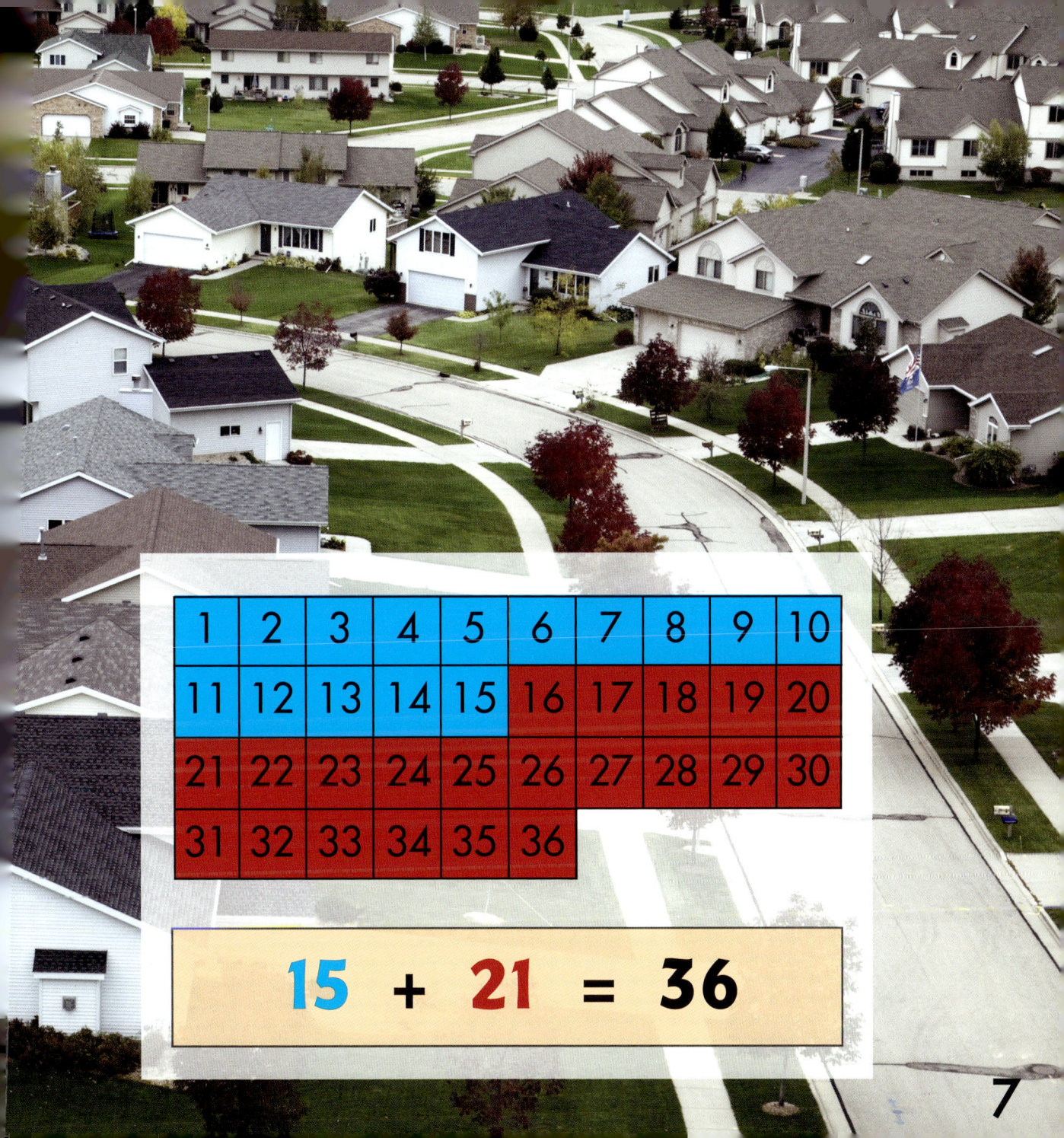

1	2	3	4	5	6	7	8	9	10
11	12	13	14	15	16	17	18	19	20
21	22	23	24	25	26	27	28	29	30
31	32	33	34	35	36				

15 + 21 = 36

Getting People to Help

Jamarie needs other kids to gather food, too.

There are 12 kids in his class.

There are 54 more kids in his school.

Jamarie asks 66 kids to help him gather food.

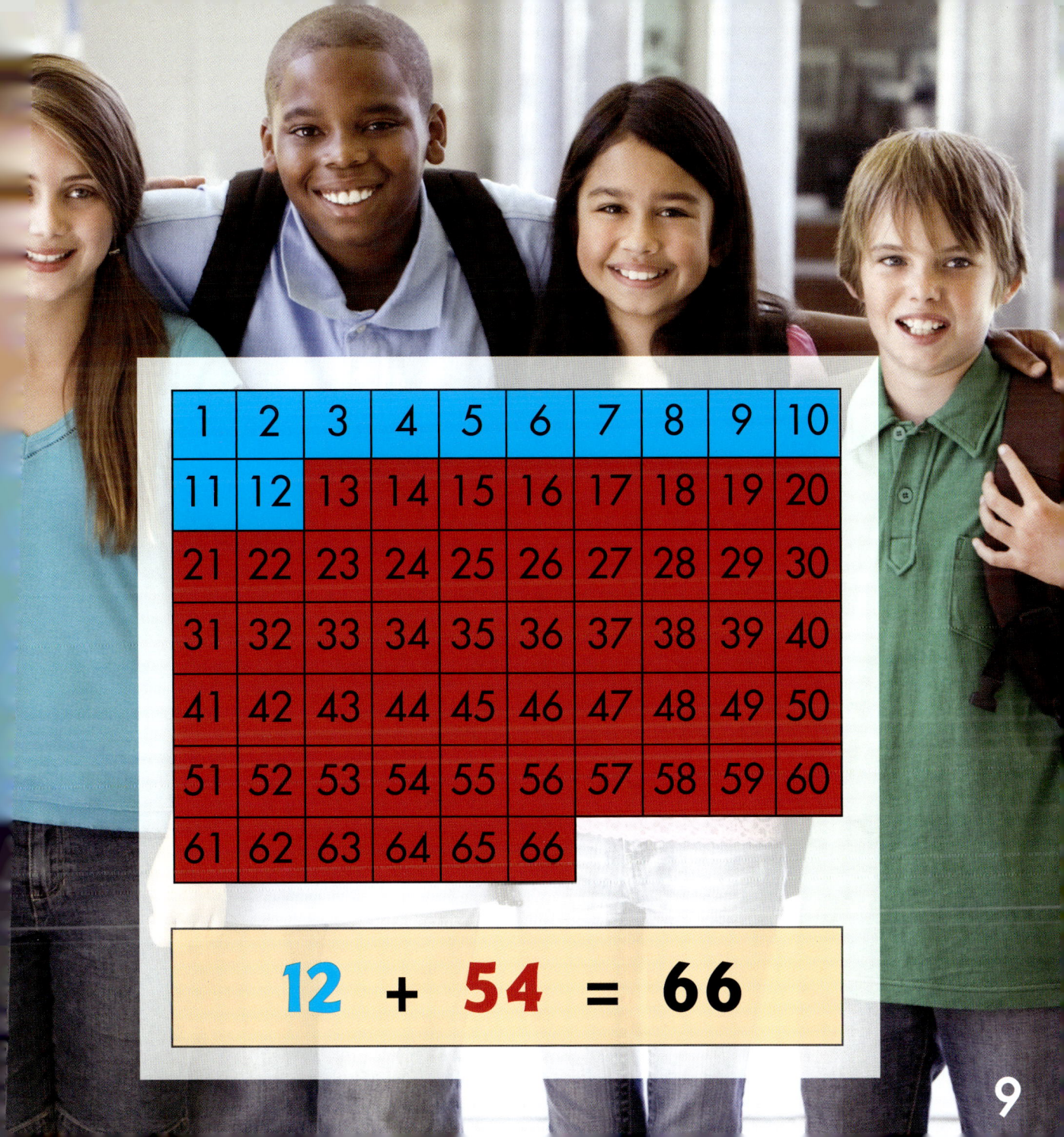

1	2	3	4	5	6	7	8	9	10
11	12	13	14	15	16	17	18	19	20
21	22	23	24	25	26	27	28	29	30
31	32	33	34	35	36	37	38	39	40
41	42	43	44	45	46	47	48	49	50
51	52	53	54	55	56	57	58	59	60
61	62	63	64	65	66				

12 + 54 = 66

Jamarie's neighbor Tom gives a lot.

He gives 23 cans of tomato soup.

He gives 17 cans of chicken soup.

Tom gives 40 cans of soup in all.

1	2	3	4	5	6	7	8	9	10
11	12	13	14	15	16	17	18	19	20
21	22	23	24	25	26	27	28	29	30
31	32	33	34	35	36	37	38	39	40

23 + 17 = 40

Sorting the Food

Jamarie sorts the food into groups.

First, he sorts the vegetables.

There are 28 cans of green beans.

There are 42 cans of carrots.

There are 70 cans of vegetables altogether.

1	2	3	4	5	6	7	8	9	10
11	12	13	14	15	16	17	18	19	20
21	22	23	24	25	26	27	28	29	30
31	32	33	34	35	36	37	38	39	40
41	42	43	44	45	46	47	48	49	50
51	52	53	54	55	56	57	58	59	60
61	62	63	64	65	66	67	68	69	70

28 + 42 = 70

Jamarie sorts the fruit next.

There are 44 cans of peaches.

There are 35 cans of oranges.

That's 79 cans of fruit.

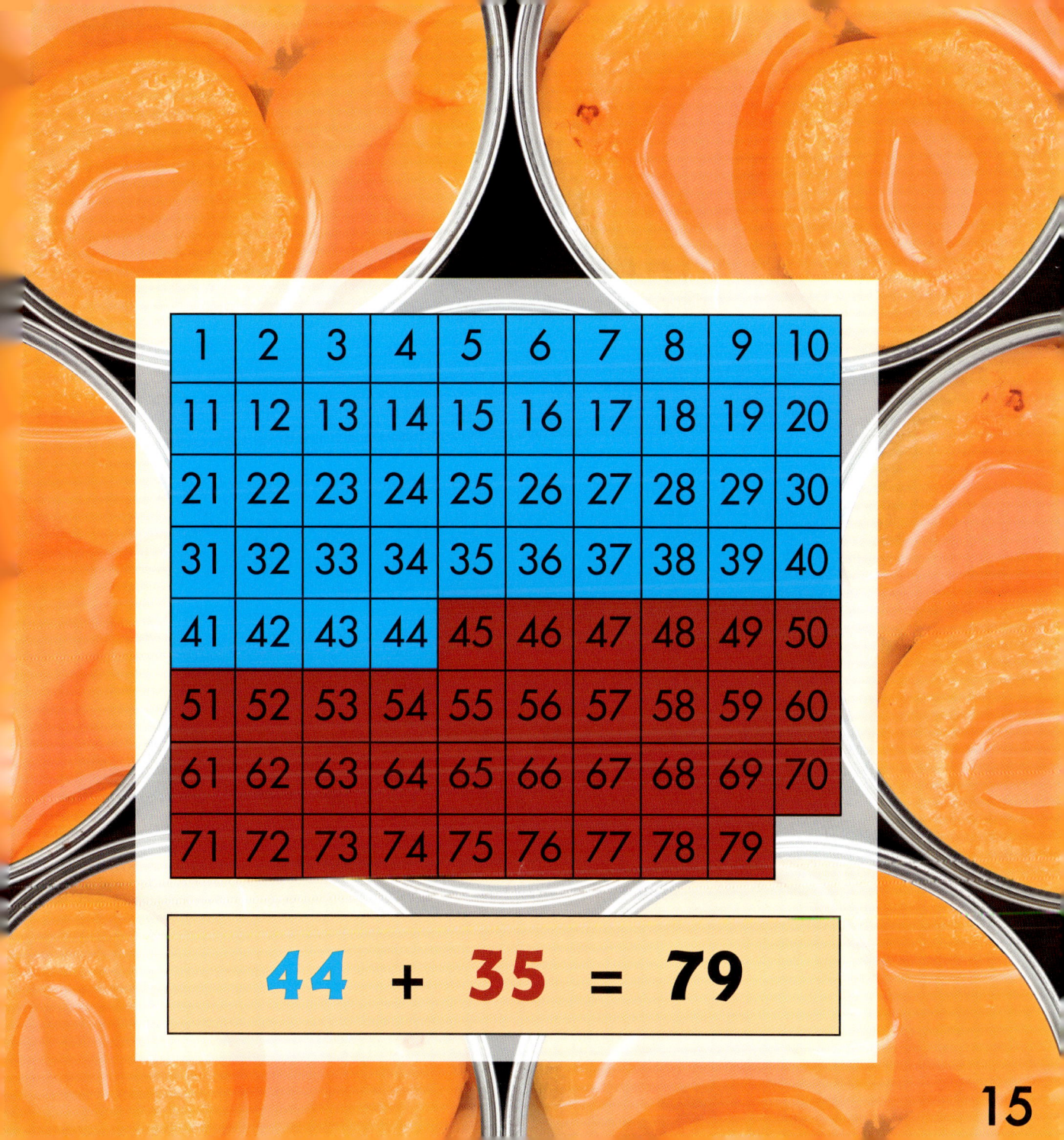

1	2	3	4	5	6	7	8	9	10
11	12	13	14	15	16	17	18	19	20
21	22	23	24	25	26	27	28	29	30
31	32	33	34	35	36	37	38	39	40
41	42	43	44	45	46	47	48	49	50
51	52	53	54	55	56	57	58	59	60
61	62	63	64	65	66	67	68	69	70
71	72	73	74	75	76	77	78	79	

44 + 35 = 79

He gathers **desserts**, too.

There are 39 boxes of cake mix.

There are 45 boxes of cookie mix.

He has 84 boxes of dessert mix.

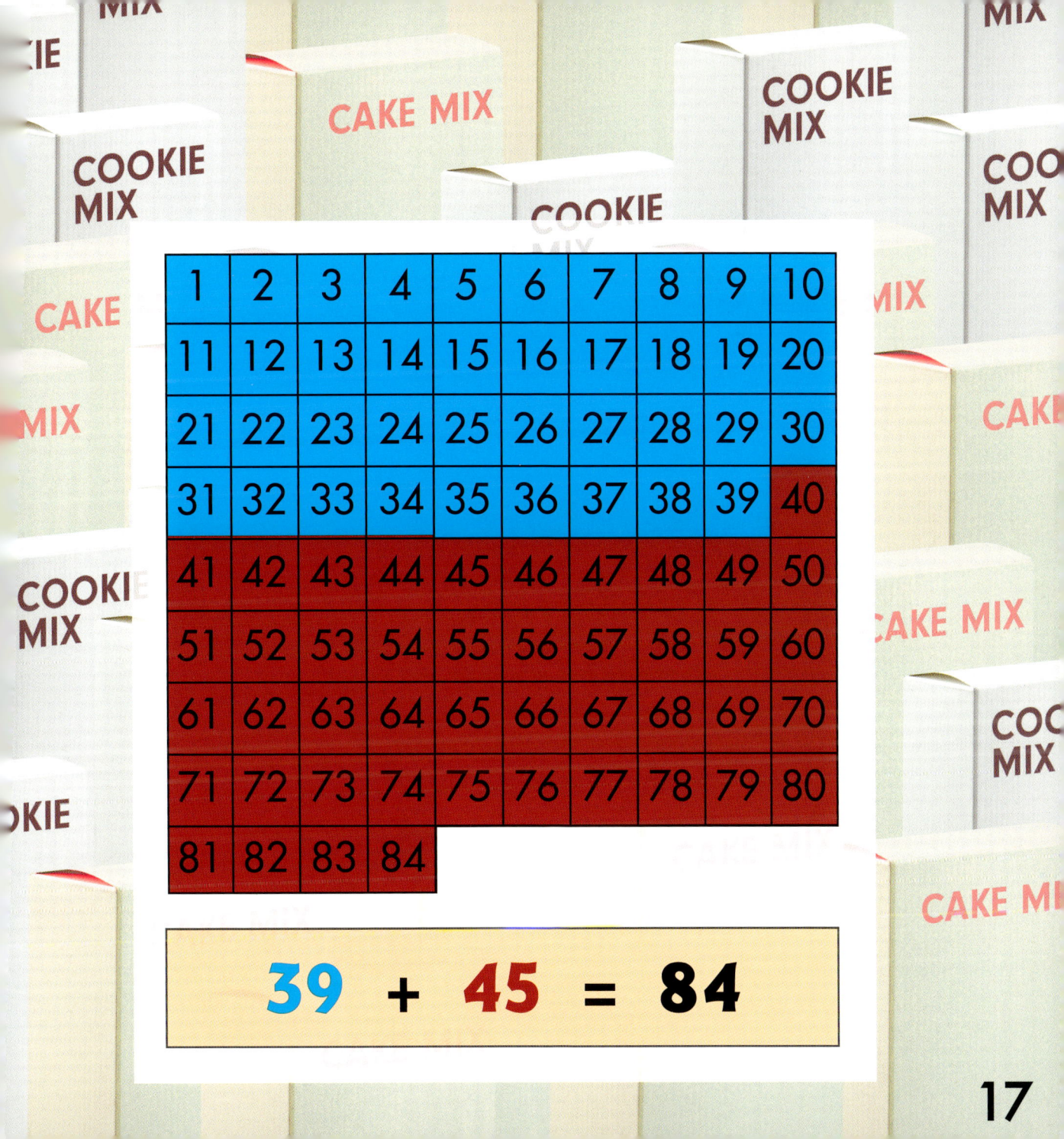

1	2	3	4	5	6	7	8	9	10
11	12	13	14	15	16	17	18	19	20
21	22	23	24	25	26	27	28	29	30
31	32	33	34	35	36	37	38	39	40
41	42	43	44	45	46	47	48	49	50
51	52	53	54	55	56	57	58	59	60
61	62	63	64	65	66	67	68	69	70
71	72	73	74	75	76	77	78	79	80
81	82	83	84						

39 + 45 = 84

Sending It Off

Jamarie needs to pack the food in boxes.

He has 41 big boxes.

He has 53 small boxes, too.

How many boxes does he have altogether?

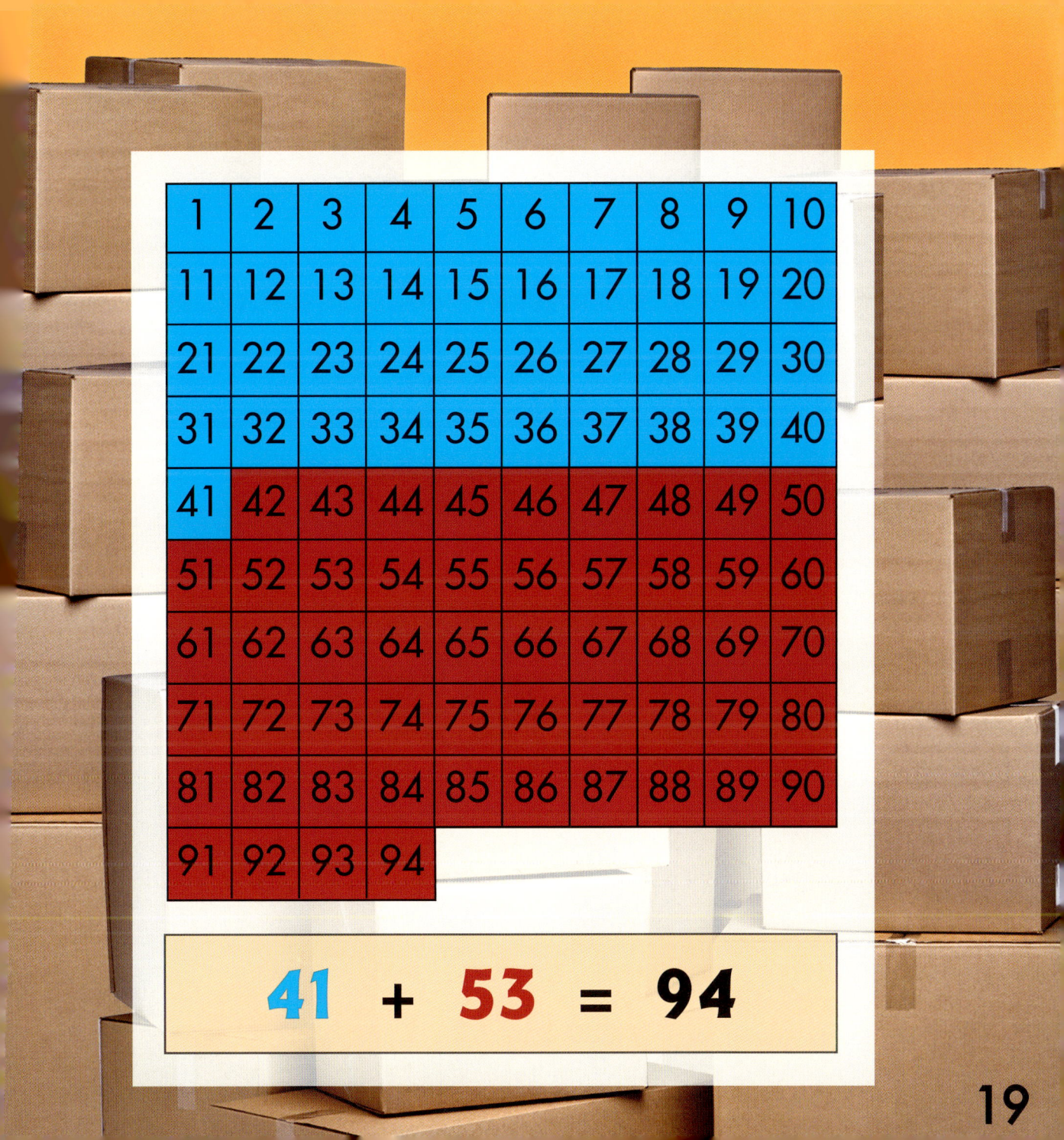

1	2	3	4	5	6	7	8	9	10
11	12	13	14	15	16	17	18	19	20
21	22	23	24	25	26	27	28	29	30
31	32	33	34	35	36	37	38	39	40
41	42	43	44	45	46	47	48	49	50
51	52	53	54	55	56	57	58	59	60
61	62	63	64	65	66	67	68	69	70
71	72	73	74	75	76	77	78	79	80
81	82	83	84	85	86	87	88	89	90
91	92	93	94						

41 + 53 = 94

Jamarie gives 40 boxes of food to the **soup kitchen**.

The other kids give 61 boxes of food

to the soup kitchen.

They give 101 boxes of food altogether.

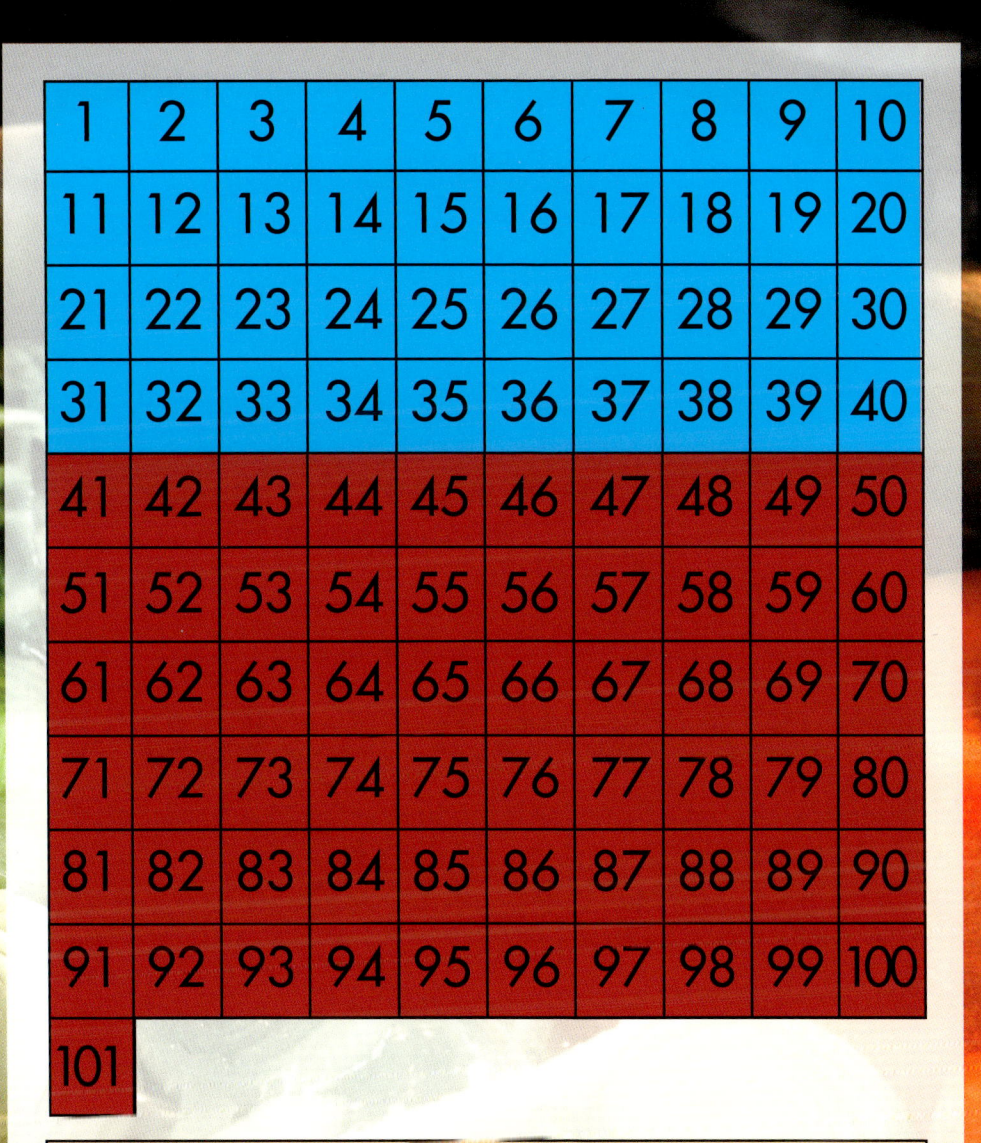

1	2	3	4	5	6	7	8	9	10
11	12	13	14	15	16	17	18	19	20
21	22	23	24	25	26	27	28	29	30
31	32	33	34	35	36	37	38	39	40
41	42	43	44	45	46	47	48	49	50
51	52	53	54	55	56	57	58	59	60
61	62	63	64	65	66	67	68	69	70
71	72	73	74	75	76	77	78	79	80
81	82	83	84	85	86	87	88	89	90
91	92	93	94	95	96	97	98	99	100

101

40 + 61 = 101

57 + 63 = 120

At the soup kitchen, Jamarie serves dinner to 57 people.

He serves dessert to 63 people.

He serves 120 people altogether.

Jamarie loves to help people in need.

Glossary

dessert (dih-ZUHRT) A sweet food eaten after a meal.

neighborhood (NAY-buhr-hood) A group of houses in the same area.

soup kitchen (SOOP KIH-chuhn) A place where people can get free food.

Index

boxes, 16, 18, 20

cans, 10, 12, 14

dessert(s), 16, 22

fruit, 14

houses, 6

kids, 8, 20

neighbor, 10

neighborhood, 6

soup, 10

soup kitchen, 20

vegetables, 12

Due to the changing nature of Internet links, The Rosen Publishing Group, Inc., has developed an online list of websites related to the subject of this book. This site is updated regularly. Please use this link to access the list: www.powerkidslinks.com/cms/nob/nfd

513.2
HAL